C000129852

Copyright 2016

By

Margaret Ogunbanwo

Published by:

WINNING FAITH

London . New York . Lagos

100 Things I wish my mother had told me!

100 Things...

I wish my mother had told me!

Margaret Ogunbanwo

Honouring mum……

Empowering daughter…

INTRODUCTION

This book has been written several times and in so many different ways in my head over the last 18 years.

If it had been taken out of that compartment all those years ago it would have read quite differently from its current form.

Having my own daughter makes me realise that although I still wish my mother had communicated a whole load of stuff to me, I must acknowledge that some things she did say back then I would not have taken notice of, and others I do not even remember.

I have also come to understand that no one can pass on what they do not know.
My mother and I chatted about the past and she acknowledges there is so much her generation didn't know, there are some things she could have told me in preparation

for life, and there are somethings she said that I just do not recall.

This book therefore is written as a lever to get the ball rolling for my girlie and other young ladies like her out there.

I realise that even now some of what I am trying to communicate may be lost in translation with age and culture differences, but this will remain as a reference journal to help her and others along her life's journey. So please feel free to share it!

The following words by the Nigerian singer/song writer Prince Nico Mbarga taken from the internet and originally written in pidgin English; summarise so eloquently how I think of my mother:

Sweet Mother
By Prince Nico Mbarga 1976

Sweet mother I no go forget you
For the suffer wey you suffer for me

Wen I dey cry my mother go carry me, she go say
My pickin wetin you dey cry yaay, yaay
Stop, stop,
Stop, stop
Stop, stop make you no cry again oh.

Wen I won sleep my mother go pet me,
She go lie me well well for bed o
She go cover me cloth, sing me to sleep
Sleep, sleep my pickin oh.

Wen I dey hungry my mother go run up and down
She go fin me sometin wey I go chop o

Sweet mother I no go forget you
For dis suffer wey you suffer for me.

When I dey sick my mother go cry, cry, cry
She go say instead wen I go die make she die o.

She go beg God, God help me

God help me my pikin oh!

If I no sleep my mother no go sleep
If I no chop my mother no go chop

She no dey tire oh……. Sweet Mother
I no go forget dis suffer wey you suffer for me.
Yaay yaay [1]

As you read this book I hope it is a help to you and other daughters you may wish to share it with, in navigating this wonderful life. May it cause you to laugh, to think ….and may it not be seen in any way as a complaint against my mother.

Translated so you, my Reader can understand, it says:
Dear mother I will never forget you,
Nor the troubles you went through for me.
When I cried my mother would carry me
Asking, "Why are you crying? Please, please stop,
Don't cry any longer!"

When I was tired my mother would cuddle me
Lay me down gently in bed, cuddle me and sing me to sleep,
Saying: "sleep well my little one."
When I was hungry my mother would run around
Looking for something suitable for me to eat
Sweet mother I will never forget you
Nor the troubles you went through for me.
When I was very ill my mother prayed and cried
Wishing that she could take my place
She would pray to God saying "please help my child,"
Don't let her die, take me instead
When I wasn't able to sleep, my mother
Couldn't sleep either, when I couldn't eat
Mother couldn't either.
She is so untiring…Dearest Mother
I will never forget the troubles
You have gone through for me.

CONTENTS

Chapter

CHAPTER 1

Pounds, Shillings and Pence

Aged 13, I commissioned this wonderful wooden money box to be made and purchased a padlock in order to secure it.

Faithfully I put in notes and coins from presents and pocket monies. I remember my delight the day I made my first 100. I had made sure that I had all crisp bank notes, and now had that *bank looking* wad that I could count in the way I had seen real bankers count!

My issues with money began, or I became aware of them when I was about 13 and wish Mama had told me…

That if I had continued my savings plan consistently with the same enthusiasm as when I started it, instead of discovering mine and other people's ability to spend, I would be swimming in money 30 odd years later. *You can take that to mean that I haven't even finished digging the pool at the moment never mind the swimming.*

My girlie is one of those born with the 'fashion shopping gene'. As the enlightened mama I have become through experience, I have shared with her how she could be debt free graduating from University; in spite of current trends, if she would begin to tithe, save and get into planned spending mode. [2]

I think, somehow, weighing that up at a young age against genetically inbuilt shopping may be that bit of information that gets put on the back burner.

Our parents always kept us informed about **the shares** they bought in our names once we were old enough to have some comprehension (did that word cause a shiver to run down your spine?). I remember getting excited while not fully understanding what a share was and when it would really be mine. Years later, and I mean years, I finally understand what a share is but I 'm still in the dark as to when they will really be mine.

Stocks and shares have been a mystery to me most of my life, always thinking those were topics for bankers and others in the financial world but not for me to comprehend. This was reinforced by the fact that Papa was a banker. Only recently am I beginning to realise that those things are accessible to all and that even a basic knowledge of them could enhance anyone's financial wellbeing greatly.

I was in my late 20's when I read my first financial newspaper: *The Financial Times* to be precise. I remember ending up with a headache because it was like trying to comprehend a foreign language in one sitting.

I was on a postgraduate course in which we were encouraged to read the trade magazines as well as the Financial Times daily. Slowly, it began to make sense, but I gave up the habit as soon as the one-year course ended. You see, my nurturing left me with the idea that I would be a homemaker and my man the provider, and as I was due to give birth to my first child and keep house there was no need to cause myself further headaches.

It is good and possible to be aware of finances and how they impact us and there are several sources, libraries, books and of course the internet that can make this easier reading, than trying to comprehend *The Financial Times* in one chunk.

I am not advocating not reading the Financial Times or literature that will enable you grow in financial intelligence of sorts, I am saying it is important that you know and have understanding of basic financial language and how money works. [2]

Keeping house in itself was an eye opener. Of course, I knew how to go to the grocery store and what ingredients to buy for food preparation, but I do wish Mama had taught me in practical and financial terms what it meant to keep house.

What percentage of money would go to rent/mortgage; what is a mortgage anyway, how much food and groceries two then three and four or more people require, what is a budget and where do you buy one, what are the best things to buy?, endless 'What's' which we now refer to as life skills. Answers to some these and other practical ideas are included in the appendices.

I have found out by trial and I mean major trials, error, indebtedness and inadvertence that:

You shouldn't spend half of all you earn on rent/mortgage. Experts recommend that not more than a third of your income should be spent on home payments whether in the form of rent to a landlord or a mortgage that enables you buy your own property.

In fact if one salary in a partnership could cover all the major expenses, then when it came time to have a child, keep the home and its contents and therefore lose one source of income, panic would not set in.

My husband and I could live on the equivalent of £25 per week in 1990 if I shopped wisely, budgeted and menu-planned.

Monies need to be set aside each month, consistently, to cover each expense including clothes and dentist costs. It never just automatically adds up at the end of each month.

Save some money each month and always have an emergency fund because stuff happens.

Do not be afraid to ask questions about how others have run successful homes and if you love reading then there are some good books out there[3]. Learn from other people's experiences quickly and early, you don't need to experience all the pain yourself. The older: be that in age or experience, should teach the younger.

I think my greatest lightning bolt was the discovery that my sweetheart and I did not think the same way about money. I think every girlie should have sessions with their partner and a financial advisor before commitment day/time, to help them formulate a plan they can both live by that incorporates their different values, or in order to create a completely new way that suits them both.

I had the notion that love meant our ideas would automatically gel in this area. In fact, I thought love would automatically make good several things, so I have included a section about love findings.

I finally understand that the quality of what I own matters more than the quantity. I come from a long line of hoarders. My home just never seemed to be un-clutter able, no matter how hard I worked. The solution that always seemed to stare me in the face was a bigger house.

I have come to realise that my wealth is not necessarily tied up with the abundance of things that I have around me. I also realise that my personal gene pool is actually one that leans towards minimalism. Contrary to what I had previously thought, I now realise that I benefit most from a spacious, uncluttered environment.

The sooner you understand what you like and have a tendency towards, the less money you will spend on trial and error and the accumulation of stuff.

I remember my first £1000 and then my second. I was about 19 and spent the first £1000 on the wings of love and the second I 'invested.' I did not understand about savings accounts and depressed economies, nor that it was possible to lose the money that I invested in that *secure* savings account.

I have never been able to recover that second £1000, as the economy of the country where my bank account was, dipped dramatically. I lost the bank details and too many years have since gone by. Having made enquiries consequently, I was advised in no uncertain terms that any such monies would have since gone towards servicing the account.

It is possible and vital to have some knowledge of basic investments and economic trends without taking up banking and being diligent at keeping your own monies as safe and secure as possible[4].

Much later in life, after the grief and pain induced by indebtedness, I read this great book that marked another turning point in my life - Debt Proof Living [2] and learnt the amazing idea that money is not first for spending, but for managing.

That the simple formula of living on 80%, saving 10% and giving away 10% of any income I received would help to secure a debt proof existence. In fact, alongside the knowledge of investment in stocks and shares, had I known this in my early 20's I could have easily joined the ranks of the worlds self-made millionaires by my 30's.

If you want things to happen, if you need to be in a position to positively influence people or if you want more flexible choices in life, you need money. To get this, you need an effective plan. The earlier in life you are able to formulate and follow this plan the better.

Money is not evil. The love of money is and it is possible to cultivate in oneself the ability to make money without being in love with it. As a result, be able to use and administer it in ways that serve a positive purpose.

A Feast is made for laughter
And wine makes life merry
But money is the answer for everything

MY WISHES

CHAPTER 2

Boys to Men and Other Ships

If memory serves me right it was the last year of junior school and I am on a roll because I am in the oldest class and arrived at the mature age of 11. The only dark cloud on my horizon was that I had received a letter requesting my parents visit the head mistress at school and I had no clue why-this was niggling.

The day finally arrives and both Mama and I return home from her having been to this meeting, the upshot of which is: I had called my friends mother an unforgivable name in our girly conversations and my friend's mother had brought the details to the head mistress' attention.

O! Was I punished severely, which to my mind then and now seems above and beyond what the "crime" deserved?

You see my friend had brought a particular piece of jewellery to school and I had made comment to the extent that it looked like something a woman referred to as '*ashewo*' wore, which in our vernacular back then was the word for prostitute.

The offence was based on the conclusion that I had called my friends Mum a prostitute. Then and subsequently I wish Mama had been more forthcoming about friendships…

I wish Mama had shared her experience of friendships and relationships early on in my younger days. You see my girlfriends and I were so committed to our relationships and our expressions of friendship so it never crossed my mind that I would ever feel betrayed by or betray any of them.

Such betrayal then seemed like a theme through my adolescence in my female to female relationships that eventually my choice of friends centred on the male of the species who I reckoned were not so emotional or unstable on a day to day basis.

Mama did tell me no boyfriends and if memory is to be believed it was the means of avoiding unwanted pregnancies. I wish that she had told me that unwanted pregnancies could also occur in any sort of relationship or dealings with my other group of friends. As in the fact that I didn't have to be dating a boy or man for that matter for pregnancy to occur with anyone of the opposite sex.

While I was good enough not to bring this upon my family my choice of male friendships above female ones meant I had to navigate a wide range of feelings and emotions with insufficient information on the subject.

The pressures of peers seek to impact us at all stages of our lives, but it appears never more so than in the teenage years. I wish I had known earlier that it is fundamental human nature to be able to choose to be who I am in spite of the dictates of peers. I wish I had known that even in the teenage years it was possible to do things as I chose even if they were contrary to my peers' latest dictates.

If awkward or uncomfortable situations arise, one quickly discovers that said peers very quickly disappear even when they had helped to bring about such situations. There is a certain freedom in being able to say, "I did it my way" and this increases the older one gets. You are free to choose.

Not everyone that crosses our path or life can be our friend. In other words, they can't all be your friends. Perhaps at this point one should consult a dictionary for the definition of friendship...A person with whom one has a bond of mutual affection, typically one exclusive of sexual or family relations.[6]

There is not the time or energy to create a bond of mutual affection with every one you meet, according to the Oxford dictionary definition of friendship.

Life certainly teaches that friends are to be categorised and that the sooner one recognises the compartment to which a certain relationship belongs the better for all involved.

Relationships can also be seasonal, so when a certain season is drawing to an end it is okay to let the friendships draw to a close also, or at least morph into a different form.

It is amazing the impact of girlie curves on relationships. One minute you are bouncing around town with your friends, the next the beat of your heart changes when you are with the group. You know that it is more to do with your favourite male pal in the group, but are not sure when this happened.

He's looking at you differently, he seems to be by your side more often and he's begun to visit you at home when the rest of the group isn't around. Is this love? As time goes by you realise that more than one male acquaintance is able to cause similar flutters or stirrings.

The change in our awareness levels is as a result of the change in those things called hormones. It does not necessarily denote love and life time exclusiveness. These like many other feelings do not last forever and therefore are not the basis upon which life time decisions should be made.

The attentions of an older, wiser, more gorgeous , more heavily loaded guy with a fab car and his own home, are not the basis of running away from the rigours of home to begin one's own supposedly less demanding and less rigorous home. That is the stuff of story books. Effort and rigour is required in any situation, perhaps just under a different guise.

While casual dating and relationships are the norm these days it is good to face up to the issues that occur with the yoyo nature of emotions in relationships.

At age 13 it is very difficult to say you know fully what you are about, as there is still a whole lot more of you to come and more life to live.

This being the case, it is even more difficult to say you know someone else well. While hormones and emotions are coming alive, they are nowhere near sufficiently developed.

In fact, they are tender shoots and thus easily crushed under the weight and demands of exclusive relationships. A stirring does not indicate a time for pursuit or the chase.

What would be better and I wish Mama had told me, is getting to know and understand these changes through observation, discussions and sharing with trusted older and wiser people who have successfully walked these paths.

The number of times I held back from doing something because none of the friends was doing it. I wish I had been told that simply by doing what I strongly desired with or without the support of the girls, I would have experienced fewer feelings of regret and remorse later on.

Someone has to be a pioneer and leader and it is fine if that someone is you! Friends may not always be around and you are an individual unit equipped with all that is needed for life: physical and spiritual. The following words by Marianne Williamson in her book A Return to Love expresses this brilliantly for me [7]:

> *We ask ourselves; who am I to be brilliant, gorgeous, talented, and fabulous? Actually, who are you not to be? You are a child of God. There is nothing enlightened about shrinking so that other people won't feel insecure around you. We are all meant to shine, as children do. We were born to make manifest the glory of God that is within us. It's not just in some of us, it's in everyone. As we let our own light shine, we unconsciously give other people permission to do the same. As we are liberated from our own fear, our presence automatically liberates others.*

A girl **can** survive being the trend setter. If you want a lifelong friendship you need to devote time and energy to the nurture of one. Distance and time do not need to result in the end of a friendship, but it takes the effort of both parties to sustain the link. Such relationships have usually gone beyond the superficial and have learnt to be flexible and adaptable. It usually requires having an understanding of one's own self as well as the other person, warts and all and a corresponding acceptance of these.

Everyone needs a friend, the form this takes may change with age, time, season of life and several other factors. Friends come in different shapes, sizes and ages. If you show yourself friendly, friends will be drawn to you.

Navigating relationships takes time and effort and therefore it is impossible to have zillions of friends while also achieving all you need and want to in life. You'll burnout!

A man of many companion's may
Come to ruin
But there is a friend who sticks
Closer than a brother

MY WISHES

CHAPTER 3

Is Catering School an Education?

I always had the potential to be top of the class, and once in a while I would be. I could not fathom a way of making this a permanent feature in my life, unlike Dad, Mama, all my Uncles and Aunties.

In fact every time the discussion of schooling and education arose in the company of parents, relations and any of their friends, they never failed to take the opportunity to drum into our consciousness how they were always in the first and second places in school and in the worst case scenario, thirds. It took us a while, but my brothers and I finally got it. Duh! They were messing with our minds. Perhaps the goal was to spur us on to aiming high, but with me it seemed like aiming was not enough.

I did not desire to be a Doctor, Nurse, Engineer, Lawyer or an Accountant, but at the time it seemed that these were the only career paths that would assure one of any level of recognition or success in the future.

It appeared as if this was the only way forward so I like many others set my sights on becoming a doctor and majored in the science subjects in senior school. I must admit that although I loved biology and thrived with this subject, Chemistry and Physics were Greek to me.

The *gyroscope* experience has followed me through life: I had read about this contraption in the then popular *Nelson and Parker* physics text book over and over, and even attempted sums and calculations based on it.

No matter what position I looked at this chapter from, the subject matter never seemed to fall into place in my brain. Some years later in a different country and school setting, I came face to face or face to gyroscope more like, with an example of the said item that I could handle and manipulate and finally it began to dawn on me about this and other seemingly complicated areas of Physics and Chemistry.

I wish Mama had told me that we don't all learn the same way. It took me training to become a teacher to realise that some need visual stimulation in order to learn effectively, while others learn by having things broken down in stages. In fact, a person's ability can be hampered by the style and type of education they are exposed to.

I desired to take up catering as a career, as both mama and grandma were excellent cooks and caterers. A glance through the secondary and university curricula failed to reveal catering as an option. If I was to

pursue this course, I would end up without a degree qualification which would be the downfall of me or so I was made to believe.
Catering was however taught and encouraged in my girl's only senior school in the domestic science lessons which was meant to be preparation for any growing female, the equivalent in the boy's only schools being wood work.

In retrospect, I would have loved to take up wood work, as I found the pace of domestic science too slow and loved the do it yourself projects. How long must it take to sew one simple outfit or cook one meal?

These days the 'real chefs', as my son calls them, are celebrities on TV with incomes comparable with that of lawyers, doctors and accountants. People who are successful and have influence are not all able to boast a university level degree, not all education is imparted in the classroom. The area of life that I have been most productive in has been catering and sometimes I can't help but wonder if I had started much earlier following the leanings of my soul rather than the changeable dictates of culture whether I would be a 'real chef'.

When I mentioned to Mama my desire to pursue a career in catering, I must admit that she did not appear very impressed and pointed me in the way of a University education instead.

Mama was a great influence in this area not wanting her girlie to miss out on a proper education.

My education has stood me in good stead and I have eventually followed the leanings of my soul. I think that it is possible to acquire an education as well as knowing and pursuing ones' souls desire at any point in life and possibly the earlier the better.

So, for the next ten years or so my love for catering was confined to helping Mama bake and to those occasions when I could convince a friend or two to allow me prepare some food for their event.

Living has revealed that being first is not necessarily an indication of level of understanding or indeed an education, although it could indicate a photographic memory or the ability to easily memorise information.

It also shows that the class room is not the only place to acquire an education, and in fact that life skills are not fully covered in formal education. Some people are not cut out for the classroom , formal education and exam settings, but have the ability to soar in their chosen career paths given the appropriate conditions.

The classroom is useful preparation for developing good habits and disciplines for living and a great spring board into the future. Success lies not only or necessarily in a chosen career, but every one carries the potential for success or failure within themselves.

Has our education opened up our minds sufficiently, in order that we can tap into that potential? If so, then it has set us on the right track.

I graduated with what I thought was a reasonable honours degree and promptly emigrated to a new country that operated different rules and systems, and I had not taken the 101 module on how to succeed with said honours degree but in a different setting.

I assumed that I had all that it took; with my graduation certificate in hand in recognition of my ability, to land that great job. So began the search for my first job. This seemed to be taking so long, and the employers I was approaching, did not seem as impressed as me by my honours degree.

I realised eventually that I lacked the information necessary to move me along in this new environment. Also that those who were more familiar with the system and were thus giving me advice, were unable to include details on how to acquire training and jobs at graduate level.

I wish Mama had told me about Curricula Vitae's (CV's) and Graduate Training schemes.

Two years down the line when we the pioneers had got better acquainted with the system, other graduate friends of ours who came to settle in the new system were better able to benefit from our hard gained experiences. They were able to start off on the correct rung on the ladder where their graduate qualifications were of more use to them than mine had been to me.

With your education get a broad range of learning, understanding and supporting wisdom so that you are better equipped to navigate any system in which you find yourself.

Ok, so I and several others dissected frogs, found out the square on the hypotenuse and understood about the weather in the Tundra regions but have since not had any use for that information.

I did not learn how to plaster a wall, manage my first salary; which by the way seemed to disappear all too quickly, or the basics of how to effectively communicate with my new boss without totally alienating myself.

There are skills that are needed if one is to be effective in the world outside of education.

These days it is so much easier to access all kinds of information through the World Wide Web www, which Mama did not have access to in her time. There are a whole range of courses on offer both hands on and those to build on the knowledge of the square on the hypotenuse should this be the way you choose to go. There are libraries and mentors that can serve as useful sources of information.

It is good to begin searching out the direction in life one wants to pursue at an early age, to be most effective on the journey of desire.

A man or woman's gift will make room for them and bring them before great men [8]. Search early in life for your talents, leanings and gifts and do all it takes to hone them, work at them, offer your services voluntarily in order to better practice your art and some day they will make an opening for you and position you in a good place.

This is not dependent on what the current career paths to success manual is suggesting is the way forward, as careers are very fluid and changeable with the times.

In more recent times I took a test in a subject I am expanding my knowledge in; following my own advice as Mama didn't know this, that it is never too late to expand ones educational portfolio. Even before I sat for the formal test I knew that I was proficient at the level in which I was sitting the exam.

The test scores supported my proficiency but I did not come away with 100%, consequently I was a bit disappointed and found myself transported back to the school setting. What was the purpose of the test and had I fulfilled it?

Some people find the idea of a test environment very daunting and therefore their results may not reflect their actual knowledge.

I had learnt that generally nothing less than being top of the class was the goal and this meant that learning became more a competition, than the acquiring and retaining of useful and retrievable information it should have been.

By all means aim to be the best but keep in mind the fact that it is about your learning for your success and that tests and exams do not always reflect what you may know. In fact, what would be a more useful exercise is to learn how to make a test reflect what you truly know and understand.

My little niece was having difficulty remembering my name, so I taught her a little rap that she still remembers today now she is no longer so little.

If I sang it I remembered it. I can still remember whole sections of songs out of the Joseph and his Technicolor coat drama that I learnt when I was in junior school. If information is in the form of music, then I seem to be able to learn and retain it more effectively.

Additionally, if I write down information I am able to better picture what was written and therefore retrieve it. When I want to absorb information most effectively I go off to a quiet place with very few people or distractions and better still very early on in the day.

I wish I had known or been encouraged to study the positive and negative trends about me as a means to being able to be a more efficient and effective me.

It is vital to study yourself as this is not only an education in itself but it helps in the pursuit of a formal education. Once you have found out what works do not hesitate to use it. Whether or not it is recommended as an acceptable way to learn is less important than if it produces in your life the results you desire.

Some of the best teaching I have received has come from looking into the Bible. I discovered first principles of management, the science of my feelings and what they are indicating and what to do with this knowledge.

I learnt about social skills and how to walk in love and forgiveness and kindness to everyone I meet. It contains information about what I think on, how to think, on friendships, marriage etc., in fact I would recommend it among one of the best handbooks for life.

Like all other information, time and energy is required to plumb its depths and find that which is useful for living.

The good thing about learning this way is that you do not need a formal setting or indeed a teacher to be able to facilitate learning.

It is all dependent on you and how much you are prepared to invest in research, listening to others to learn from their experiences, as well as engaging the learning in a manner that facilitates your most efficient assimilation of the information acquired.

Choose my instruction instead of
Silver
Knowledge rather that choice gold

MY WISHES

CHAPTER 4

The Metamorphosis

Red jean trousers! I can see them in my mind's eye even today. I was 14 years old and was convinced I fitted into a dress size 14.

Mama comes back from her trip with the long awaited red skinny jeans, and shock horror to find I wasn't what I thought I was! No matter what I tried those trousers would not fit, they went up for sale in Mama's hairdressing salon and with the proceeds I would try to get a pair that fit me. That day scared me for life. I wish Mama had told me...

That unlike my sister I was not born with the skinny genes nor apparently for the skinny jeans. I was going to have to do things very differently in order to look anything like my sister.

Perhaps I wasn't meant to look like my sister. I have learnt that two people can eat seemingly similar amounts and end up looking very different.

If I was going to be the longed for dress size 14 then I would have to seek for a different approach to food more suited to my gene pool. I had heard of diets but even back then I could not convince myself that I could sustain one of these long term.

I read another good book that marked another turning point in my life called; *Free to be Slim* by Neva Coyle and Marie Chapian.[10] You would think perhaps I have come to understand that a good way for me to learn is through the medium of reading.

A statement that hit home and has stayed with me since then is that I am responsible for what goes into my mouth! As is the case with money, a person's feeding habits and tendencies need to be understood and managed for optimum output.

The things I liked and craved for most were those causing me the greatest problem. I was not doomed for life to continue to consume these. I could retrain myself to eat differently and even to like black eyed beans. I could find ways of cooking different foods so they were more palatable to me.

Exercise, especially the ones I enjoyed were ok. I recall having to get a note to be let off physical education in school because when I went from hot to cold or vice versa suddenly I came out in bumps that were unbearably itchy. Later, I discovered these were called hives.

I would internalise all my heat and feel I was internally combusting. This became my escape route from the dreaded physical education (PE) and entrance into a world of unfitness. If I was the PE teacher would I have believed the internal combustion story? Although it was true it was not impossible to overcome through slowly warming up and approaching PE slightly differently from the rest of the class.?

How I look is important but does not define me. Clothes and accessories can only help to reflect who I truly am they do not make me. I think I heard this one several times through my developing years but was sceptical.

I thought it was an excuse used by those who didn't quite look the predefined part. Again there is the need to understand oneself and sense of style and fit one's appearance to this and not to the latest fad or to peer pressure.

A good friend of mine once said and I have quoted again and again," if the house needs paint then paint it!" Make up is one of those useful tools that can be used to enhance and hide. Use it and don't let it make a clown of you.

The older one gets depending on the skin type, environment and a range of other factors there maybe the greater need for make-up. Young skin is so fresh and beautiful that it only takes a little make up to showcase what already exists.

What is important here is the ability to get the relevant advice and products that suit. An aunt said to me in my early twenties that it was important when young to use good quality make up or no make-up at all rather than use cheap products that only serve to damage the skin.

Our physical appearance changes with the times and seasons, some changes we can influence and these we need to understand and control. Others we can do very little about and at this point a girlie must understand that her person consists of more than just a physical body. While the body morphs with age and not always in an upward direction (no pun intended) the mind has the ability to sharpen with time and experience, providing one with valuable wisdom and a voice.

A girlie and ultimately a woman needs to live in the fullness of herself and take pleasure and pride in all facets of her make up. She needs to appreciate herself for who she is, which includes her spirit, her soul and her body.

I caused my Mama some frustration in my late teens as I had 'got religion' and my physical appearance was of very little concern to me. I was clean and tidy but I refused to add to my dressing any form of adornment. You see, in the early teens, there had been the unbreakable law instituted by Mama about no makeup or adornment for me.

I wish Mama had told me at what stage the rules changed and why. Perhaps her insistence that I wear some make up at age 19 was meant to be the indicator for me that things had changed, a new phase had commenced in my life that required some enhancement. Indeed, things had changed, because I had begun creating my own rules and one of them was that if anyone was going to fancy me it would be as I was and not as I appeared with adornment.

Somewhere between early and late teens I did wear make-up outside the realm of Mama's sphere of influence, when she wasn't there to see me.

If I took a deep look I could admit that the main reason to modify my looks in my younger days was in order to appear even more attractive to those around me especially the boys. I wish I could have discussed and understood this part of my life more with Mama, my drives, motivations and the way she saw things.

I am still of the opinion that it is good for the natural state of me to be that on display generally.

I recall many a lady who was concerned about the first time she would be viewed by her love without the face. Would he still like me? Make-up is appropriate at certain times, ages and seasons of life, but again it does not define who we are but is meant to be an appropriate means to an end.

Charm is deceptive, and beauty is fleeting; But a woman who fears the Lord is to be praised

MY WISHES

CHAPTER 5

Cupid and Her Ways

I am lying in the nook between mine and my sister's single beds, being quiet but very alert to sounds around me, especially that of the room door being opened. You see Denise Robins was holding my interest at that moment.

The problem was that she was not legal tender for me and even though I had got her down from the book shelf in Mama's room, I had been told that I was too young to read these types of novels.

In addition, I added Mills and Boon and Barbara Cartland to the mix so from the age of about 11 to about 18 I received a concise education in the ways of Cupid or the state of being 'in love' from these novels.

You see Mama did tell me not to read the books, at least not at too early an age but I wish she had told me about love!

Mills and Boon, Denise Robins-I remember not being allowed to read these but must confess I read every single copy of my Mum's Denise Robins novels and lost count of the number of Mills and Boon's. Every month some pocket money was set aside for the newest title. There was an exchange programme active at school also, so many of us were buying into the happy, romantic endings in these novels.

I must admit that at the time there were few if any African writers publishing in this romantic genre, so all us M+B (Mills and Boon) fans were longing for a westernised kind of romance as defined in our manuals. The problem was the guys were not reading the same manuals.

Novels, movies and peers were the main learning ground on issues of love. Time has shown that the basis of a lot of this tuition was and is fantasy.

Mama didn't tell me I couldn't run my fingers through African type hair. When I finally worked this out I vowed to marry a European with long flowing hair.

How many people could you fall in love with in a year, at the same time and at what age?

You see the "tingly" feelings of excitement and arousal had begun. What was shocking was that after a month of longing after one gorgeous hunk and feeling like one could never love another, Mr. Even-More-Gorgeous would come along and new previously un-experienced tingles would develop.

Help Mama, what's going on with me? Who should I choose or more to the point at that time, who would choose me?

I was instructed- No boyfriends till you are older! The reasons and the term older were never clearly defined. I do recall that the brothers had brought home girlfriends who were my peers. One rule for me and one for them I wondered?

I wish Mama had explained more about emotions and how fickle they could be. How they grew and matured and how novels were written solely for the purpose of generating income and not as a basis for my reality.

I wish someone had told me that the rules that existed for one sex and not the other were not necessarily based on anything more than societal and cultural dictates. These dictates are ever changing, when I crossed country borders the cultural norms changed. It is best for a person's values to be based and rooted in one's foundational beliefs rather than societal and cultural norms.

Increased responsibility, stress, childbirth and rearing along with several other factors have an impact on love. Their impact starts with the feelings, but be assured that this does not indicate that love is dead.

Remember love is not just a feeling. Sometimes lives can be so fraught and preoccupied that one may be tempted to ask in the style of Tina Turner: What's love got to do with what I am doing? At this time all love needs is a little coaxing, some relaxation and a determined re-focus. Holidays especially relaxing ones are a good way of rediscovering errant love.

I must tell you about love and money. More than anything Mama should have told me about this one, because the shock factor here is so great it could turn one's hairs grey. When cupid strikes one of the most important and vital things that should be looked at, turned over, explored and discussed is the money question.

This should be done way before commitment and if you can't face the heat, get out of the kitchen quick! Apart from perhaps sex, I am aware of no greater love killer than the money issue. Current marriage and divorce statistics appear to support my view. Money can be a strain on that undying love and has been known to kill love dead.

As this is a potentially explosive area it may be handy to discuss this topic in group situations, with money counsellors present or with someone who has lived to remain in love and is thriving.

Love and sex are two completely different things. It is possible and common place really for sex to occur without love.

One of the most common effects of love is sexual relationship. You do not need to entangle your soul in sexual ties, bonds and relations with everyone and anyone on the path to love. There is nothing that says that maturity equates to sexual freedom. As girlies turned Nan's will tell you there is a lifetime of opportunity before you to practice sex and many have been known to run out of steam early in life.

Again I say do not mix love up with sex and it is well OK to pace one's sexual experience. It is not dumb, not to have experienced what one's peers have at 13, 14, and 15 (see chapter on ships). It's alright to follow your foundational beliefs and pioneer the way. Stay the pace and be enjoying love and sex into your golden years!

Chinese, Australians, Africans; you better believe it; love can strike out of any tribe or nation. A person's birth place; while it influences their beliefs, is not a basis for accepting or indeed denying love. It is always a help to understand the background of the person you fall in love with, even if it is the boy next door from the same village or settlement as your parents.

In some cultures, parents research backgrounds. It is expedient to understand where each person is coming from before commitment day.

We were groomed by our culture. In mine women folk were groomed for marriage, this was the next step. The rites of passage went something like: teenage, 21, university, marriage then children and you are on your way to achieving nirvana. As a result, one of my top most goals was to achieve this state of euphoria promised by the books, mags, TV, other women and mothers.
I wish Mama had talked me through the many other goals that I could have set my sights on in addition.

In my teenage years I remember exchanging definitions of love with my girlfriends The following one has stayed with me and causes me to chuckle each time I think of it.

Love is a feeling you feel when you feel a feeling you have never felt before. Duh!

There it is and pretty much defined how we related around love. It was not the common thing to have Mums sit around and discuss love with their girlies. If you mentioned the word sex then it was time for big trouble, and even if you mentioned it around Aunty it would usually get back to Mum that there was a loose girl in the house.

I so wish I could have talked with Mama about feelings. I grew up with the understanding that this kind of talk or exploration was taboo. Girly love is more than a feeling and goes beyond a good looking rich person who can support your life's dreams. And it certainly should not be blind.

Love is patient, love is kind. It does not envy, it does not boast, it is not proud. It is not rude, it is not self- seeking; it is not easily angered, it keeps no record of wrongs. Love does not delight in evil but rejoices with the truth. It always protects, always trusts, always hopes always perseveres. Love never fails. [12]

If you ask me love is a tough call, not a feeling. Love is not for the immature to take on, it requires some grit, determination and the making of hard choices.

So when you come to choose, do so in the light of the above definition of love.

Delight yourself in the Lord
And He will give you the desires of
Your heart [13]

MY WISHES

CHAPTER 6

The Art of Organisation …A Place Called Home

No matter how hard I tried I never seemed able to keep my half of the room looking like my sisters'. I concluded that she was born with the *tidy gene* and I was totally lacking the said gene.

My mother didn't buy that one and I can hear her saying even now,"… Maggie go and tidy your room O!" I wish Mama had told me.

My sister and I were born with different tendencies and I was not the bad one because I was not able to keep my many possessions under control.

The motivation for tidying my room could never be in order to be like my sister, but rather, that I would be better able to find those keys, socks, books and other such items that always seemed to be missing (Ah where me phone, ah where me keys?). My sister by the way never seemed to have a problem locating her things.

I do not think I made the connection until in my 30's when I read this wonderful book, Sink Reflections by Marla Cilley-The Fly Lady [14] that saved my sanity and my home from being condemned as a civic amenity site otherwise called a dump.

I did not have to keep everything I acquired including the packaging, 54 skirts, 74 tops; some of which I was too 'chubby' to fit into, to mention but a few. I discovered it was ok to give things away, if it was faded I didn't have to keep it and that favourite skirt with the hole in could be replaced by another favourite item of clothing.

I shouldn't start on the cute packing boxes, ribbons, wrapping paper and the other things I squirreled away as I just knew I would have need for them some day.

It is very difficult to keep a cluttered space tidy and airy, unless you have servants to do the work, access to unlimited storage space and loads of money to acquire a new space once the present one is filled up.

The art of organisation could be learnt by anyone, especially those not born with the instinct. I have to write myself a cleaning schedule to keep my house in order. This works for me and is OK.

I heard a genetically tidy friend of mine say one day that she had a place for everything. What a light bulb moment that was for me! In spite of this, it was still some years later when I finally comprehended that if I always put my keys in a designated place then I would not have to look for them frantically every time I needed them. They would always be where I put them and this applies to most other immobile property.

The truth of the matter was that things remained where I put them but as there were so many things, piles and places, I could never remember without frantic searching, where the particular urgently required item was stowed.

For as long as my memory serves me, growing up we always had some kind of paid house help including a nanny, cook, 'washer man', driver, cleaning person and if all else failed, Grandma was there on hand to produce delicious meals. The shock that set in for me when I realised my role in my home required me to fulfil all these positions myself is indescribable.

The problem, as I see it, is Mama had not informed me that the help in our home was not the norm in every household or culture and would certainly not be my norm in the future.

What did I know about wash days, to-do lists and menus, [app 3] especially as I hated the repeated menus that we had week in week out through some periods of growing up in Mama's home? The idea that a menu could be a useful tool for me didn't cross my mind.

It got really complicated when I had stacks of neatly or not so neatly arranged piles of letters waiting for me to take action. Some of them I am sure waited over a year.

Until, that is, I heard executive sharing tips at a seminar that had been useful in helping him fulfil his demanding role in the office." I deal with my mail immediately", was the statement that blew my mind!

It was common sense and so simple, why hadn't anyone told me this before? Maybe that particular sense is not so common after all.

Don't get me started on the dusting, the cleaning, gardening, cooking, shopping and children...argh! Mama hadn't passed on the manual that had helped her manage her environment so immaculately.

I must admit that when I had to do chores at home, she let me know I had to do them for the sake of my future, what she didn't add was how this all came together to produce a positive end result.

Sink Reflections saved and rescued me, along with other good books out there in the market, as well as picking up tips from people who had achieved the results I desired.

I learnt the pioneer's way; that it was not a function of birth or gender to know these things, and there was no shame in asking. Asking only served to increase my knowledge of how to navigate life more effectively.

We always had someone to do the repairs and the daily maintenance in the house. Neither one of my brothers, nor I or my sister had previous cause to acquire any do-it-yourself skills.

During my fun-filled days in further education, when groups of guys would talk about painting their rooms, I would get very excited at the idea; however, I never got the opportunity to help or practice, to be more precise, as this was something the male only of the species did according to the unwritten norms of the time.

While serving my country in a year out stint of National Youth Service, we were involved in digging up street gutters or drains in a part of town that needed them. I so loved and enjoyed this exercise, but was the only female on the team who would engage with the spade and pitch fork.

You see the other sensible girls had learnt that this was not a job for the female of the species, but obviously I hadn't been paying attention during that lesson.

Culture shock set in when I transferred living allegiances "overseas" and DIY was the norm! It took me years and then some to work out that doing something I enjoyed and had the potential to be good at was not stepping outside my pre-defined role or stepping on my other half's toes.

It was neither macho for a woman to DIY nor effeminate for a man to be efficient in the kitchen.

In fact, cultures are so fluid that today most of the celebrated chefs in Europe are male.

I wish Mama had taken me through the session about ability and skill, desire and affinity. About how to lay bricks, seal cracks, replace toilet seats along with other minor

DIY projects I have had reason to grapple with along the way.

These days there are so many self-help and craft books by people who happily share their knowledge; there is also that source of all information - the internet, as well as short courses in just about every subject. Whether the project is knitting or bricklaying anyone can try their hand at anything at least once.

Culture and gender do not necessarily have to narrow one's options. It is OK to break out of the mould, as history has proved. For when it suits, one mould will be very quickly discarded for another without a second thought anyway.

A wise and experienced friend once said; and I paraphrase as total recall is less than perfect these days..." You work so hard to acquire things that you are too old to utilise or enjoy when the hard work is over" i.e. retirement.

There are different phases in our lives, or seasons as we popularly refer to them these days.

For most people, the longer they interact with this world, that is the longer they live the more opportunity they have to live the life they have envisioned.

I wanted a home like Mama's or at least like my favourite Auntie's Neither Mama nor Aunty started out with the things I saw and perceived as desirable at age 19.

It is possible to have and maintain a nice space at any phase in life and within your current budget. It is ok not to be driven by other people's definitions of what a modern space should look like in the teens, 20's, and 30's or at any stage in life.

It is smart to ride out the current season within the available budget, indeed it requires some research, hunting and looking around for bargains and shopping smart.

It is amazing what you can find around you and in other people's cast offs that can serve a useful purpose for you. Shabby chic or upcycling I think are the new terms.

It is not only acceptable but useful to healthy living to design and live in one's space within one's budget.

It's fine for your space to reflect your own tastes and style. We are not bound by any rules of design and spatial appearance and should not be so bogged down by what is defined as acceptable.

You see those who have chosen to redefine style according to their own instincts or taste suddenly become the design icons of the day. Feel free to search for and follow your own style and define your space by it, after all, you are the one who has to live in it.

Bend the rules and observe how things appear because if you don't, someone else will, and take all the credit and accolades, becoming the next guru instead of you.

We had a menu which must have made life easier for Mama, what with her busy schedule; the issue was it was the same week in week out. It was so predictable and had become boring that we looked forward to food gifts from friends and neighbours as well as the ever present party invitations.

The catch was if a food gift came from a non-approved source it was back to the menu. Well menu planning does not have to be difficult to do or boring for those who have to follow it.

The following tips may help you get going:
Tip: Start by making a list of all your favourite foods under the headings of Breakfast, Lunch and Dinner. Keep this list safe and add to it as your favourites expand.

If you have a family, write down their favourites, if you are like me, you may have over 30 items on the list. If not, don't panic! Just add to it as your culinary tastes and experiences expand.

Tip: Break down the days of the week into food types. For example:

Monday   - Rice dish
Tuesday   – Pasta
Wednesday – Potatoes
Thursday   -Cultural
Friday   - New cuisines
Saturday   - Leftovers
Sunday   -Roast dinner

Other options include African dishes, International cooking, Old Time favourites, Fish dishes, Vegan meals Mince Beef dishes and so on.

The first time you under take this exercise, it may be time consuming, but once done it makes life so simple and time efficient, it is well worth it.

In addition, it relieves some of the pressure of shopping and deciding what to eat tonight by allowing you write a grocery shopping list [app 4] and also helps with budgeting. Life is not so rigid so you can chop and change, if you choose too.

If you have over 30 recipes, you can plan for more than 30 days at a time and not repeat the same menu item more than once every 60 days. This will certainly take the boredom of repetition out of cooking and eating.

When looking for a home along with the considerations of money and location, it is a good idea to consider what you want from a home.

Do you want to do minimal cleaning, avoid too many surfaces and nooks, do you want different spaces for different functions and so on? Then you certainly don't want an old property with 17 rooms, or perhaps you do? You have to consider the suitability of a property on the basis of what function you want from it.

Your present home may not be your ultimate dream pad but it could be a small reflection of what you would like. So, do the exercise, understand what you want out of a home and then armed with that knowledge, go looking within your price range.

Unless the Lord builds the house
Its builders labour in vain. [15]

MY WISHES

CHAPTER 7

Legally Binding Documents

He was going to be tall, dark and handsome, but most especially he would be of Caucasian heritage so that he could have long flowing hair through which I could run my fingers.

There is a power in regularly reading the written word and in my case the Romantic Novels of the time helped me to form a picture in my mind of the ideal man.

I was always going to be married, this I knew to be part of my destiny, Mama and Grandma and almost everyone else made reference to my future in the context of being married and having my own husband. I wish I knew…

I certainly knew that I was being groomed to run my husband's home, so all the housekeeping lessons that I, but not my brothers had to undertake, were to ensure a good future for me in my husband's home.

I wish Mama had told me that marriage was not mandatorily the next goal I had to fulfil in life after my first degree. The environment and culture in which we were raised made it appear as if this was officially the next step to undertake after studying, on the journey of life.

In fact, I think that my goals stopped here for a while. What could be better than getting the man of one's dreams, getting bound for life and then settling into the role of being the best for him?

Though I could see that not all the marriages around me seemed to deliver that promise, I with the help of my favourite novelists, was convinced that this was the culmination of my life's training.

I slowly began to meet others who had as their next goal travelling round the world, or getting a PhD, or going to work as a missionary somewhere and must admit that I thought they could not be serious! How could they give up the promise of marriage for these other things first?

It truly would have been nice to know that I could have followed other paths in life first without missing out on marriage.

I knew marriage was a lifetime commitment but was still happy to go ahead with it at an early age. This indeed was my programming. I say to my girl and wish mama had said to me, that because of the nature of marriage it is vital to make an informed choice.

You don't just marry what you see, the great dark looks and hair, but the person and all in their life to date that has been involved in making them the person they have become. An understanding or at least some knowledge of a person's home life and background from a number of different sources, like their friends, family social media profile is a valuable indicator of who and how a person is.

Help in making this choice is invaluable and preferably not from the latest soap on TV or novel. It is also useful to have a level of understanding and maturity as these are required to build a successful relationship, living in such close proximity with someone else.

Marriage is not just another goal on the path of a girl's life but is something that requires thought and research. Very little is hidden from the other person in the marriage relationship. No one else out there may be aware of your idiosyncrasies, but living so closely within a marriage relationship means that you can't hide them from your partner who has access to you and everything about you.

It requires some level of understanding of oneself and one's nature as a human being; your likes and dislikes, how you react in and to different situations, whether you are an introvert or extrovert, to be able to understand another person's nature.

I wish I had known that it was neither my responsibility nor would I able to be the solution to anyone else's life even the one I loved with all my heart. I could not always make them happy, nor could I always walk the path they had to walk.

In spite of the desire to create the perfect haven for my husband and family to dwell in there was something in me that longed for more than simply doing that. I had creative ideas and thoughts that needed an outlet outside my immediate sphere, but these conflicted with my preconceived ideas of what marriage should look like, and ultimately resulted in me having feelings of guilt. I felt even more guilt when I realised that my idea of a haven and my husband's where at some points, divergent.

Mama where are you? All this guilt, all the dichotomy, why are things occurring this way? I have come to realise that whilst we are in a legal, loving and nurturing relationship each of us has a responsibility coupled with choice, to live and think for themselves, and to make the best of the gifts and talents with which we are naturally endowed.

The great designer did not intend us to be replicas of each other. I'm sure that if he did he would have made us so right from the start. We are made to complement each other. Our gifts and talents are there to enrich us as individuals, in our marriages and in our communities.

Such guilt and angst as I went through can be avoided by better understanding what marriage is and by looking openly, with your intended, at what each of you is bringing to the relationship, and most, if not all of this, before marriage. To legally bind oneself to another is not child's play.

Get to know both yours and his strengths and weaknesses and build your lives around these so that you complement each other, rather than follow the dictates of culture, environment and current acceptable norms.

It may not be the acceptable thing for the female to go out to work while the man looks after the home or and children because that is where you find yourselves in life, but does it work for you both? Is it in agreement with your beliefs and values? Who handles the money is that automatically any one person's role or is one of you a 'whizz' in this area?

It is important that you find what works for you within your own value system and in spite of the many clamouring opinions.

Build your own home, as you and your partner are the ones who have chosen each other and are the ones that will have to live with the consequences of your choices once you make your commitments and the door is shut.

Two years into marriage, the tingly feelings that had been so prevalent in my pre-marriage days went missing. When I searched a bit deeper, I realised that they had been waning for a while.

This concerned me no end so I did a quick poll among friends and others and felt even further that I had a problem which was uniquely mine.

Again I was directed to another book that helped my thinking. In his book The Five Love Languages by Gary Smalley [16] the author was talking about how things change pre-marriage and post marriage. I eventually found out later in life that I was not unique in feeling this but that maybe I was the only one brave enough to express it, or perhaps others had not got to that stage in their relationships.

I wish someone had told me that the absence or presence of tingles is not an indicator of love, nor is it the definition of love.

In fact, it would have been helpful to know that a whole load of things could induce similar tingles and that being committed to one person did not mean that I was never going to feel similarly for anyone else. Loving commitment is what keeps one focussed on the choices made, is what keeps one talking and relating through dirty nappies, insufficient income and all those other potential things that may arise that no one mentioned could happen in a relationship.

I know many a girlie looks forward to sexual fulfilment and that these days it is uncool to delay sexual gratification. There is a whole life time of opportunity ahead. Many females seem to go through a period when it is no longer such a priority. There is no need to start too early and reach burn out early.

There is very little benefit in experimenting with different subjects as this leads to a basis for comparison and dissatisfaction.

Sex is a deep expression of intimacy and rather than Mamas saying to girlies, "Don't do it," the truth is that waiting to express deep commitment is gratifying and does not reduce one to running around seeking for the ultimate sexual fulfilment and ending up disillusioned and being called all kinds of unsavoury names.

Marriage, like most other commitments takes time and energy and doesn't just happen. It takes determined focus and requires self-control, maturity, understanding and a whole number of other adjectives.

I was convinced that loving and being loved was all that it would take, but realise that committing for life to someone else is akin to new metal machinery that with the help of a lot of grease, and wear over time, will operate optimally. The metal shavings and sparks that accompany initial use is not an indication that the machinery is not suitable rather that time is needed for it to bed in and settle.

Similarly, the rubbing against each other and the sparks flying in a relationship, though disconcerting and often painful are not indicators of a bad marriage.

How is it possible that housework, pregnancy, childbirth, holidays to name a few, can dictate the direction of a marriage. All these things come with their own demands and stresses. In situations where there is no understanding or agreement about them, resentment and lack of fulfilment can build up. This in turn leads to lack of mutual enjoyment of the relationship.

From a girly who was nurtured to care for her future home, I found that Mama had omitted to tell me that the things I was taught would help create a good home were also areas with the potential to place stress on a loving relationship.

No one had explained that the onset of pregnancy might affect sexual drive, or that distress in childbirth could have an impact on the sexual and other areas. How could taking out the bins, washing the cars and other such mundane things adversely affect such a deep commitment?

I wish Mama had told me that not everyone teaches their children to iron their bed linen before making up the bed. This would have saved me and my hubby hours of grief; what with me expecting him to ensure that any sheets that we used on our beds had to be freshly laundered and ironed. In fact, I wish I had just known, that it was not only possible but safe and acceptable to lay on sheets that hadn't been ironed.

I must say that not only Mama but several books, specialists, friends and well-wishers mentioned the C word.

Communication is all important! What they all left out is that communication is more than just talking. It is possible to talk with someone who lives in an African desert about snow but this does not mean they will comprehend or understand what has been communicated enough to make use of the information.

One must be able to explore communication and preferably before commitment, in order to establish that each person understands where the other is coming from and going to. In order to ensure they will be able to continue to do so perhaps even more effectively with time.

It is said this way in a quote I like, "How can two walk together except they be agreed?" [17]

The wedding day is just the beginning of the rest of your lives together. Start as you mean to go on. If you intend to have the most lavish dream of a day at yours and the banks expense remember that you will wake up to that fact the next day when all the guests have gone home.

What one wears and who is on the guest list is much less important than what one says on that day. I realise it may not be fashionable in some circles to use the term 'for better, for worse in sickness and in health till death do us part' - these days; but that is what is being said in effect.

To make this promise to only one person is something not to be entered into lightly or based on dark good looks, tingly feelings, peer pressure, societal demands or any other temporal influence inside or outside oneself.

Do two walk together unless they have agreed to do so? [17]

MY WISHES

CHAPTER 8

Welcome to The Hood!

I wanted four of them and preferably in two sets of twins. The culture in which I was raised had this folklore about eating specially prepared twins beans, so I stuffed myself appropriately with these as often as the opportunity arose.

I had also researched and found that I was in the right pedigree both in my family and my husband's family histories for the increased possibility of having twins. Finally, I had prayed and was set for my first experience of parenthood and more specifically motherhood and all it entailed.

From everything I had seen and heard, as soon as I desired children of my own and did the necessary things, they would come.
I was ready and doing all that I needed for this to happen and two years later nothing had happened. T

hen several expensive tests later I was convinced I saw a clear blue. I waited in anticipation for the bulge that I was so looking forward to, to grow.

Two to three miscarriages later, after loads of heart searching and guilt trips I finally began to grow a bulge under the watchful eye of the doctors and consultant.

How tiring and draining and so far from my initial understanding of the child birthing process. It was also seemingly unique to me as all my friends were doing well and on to their second time around.

When my girly was born everyone who saw her for the first time, cooed over how beautiful she was. I did not see this initially all I could see was this scrunched up little warm bundle that I instantly fell in love with.

The love so engulfed me that for a while I didn't want another child as I was convinced I had no more love left to give.

I don't recall Mama and I having the discussion about how many you could love equally at a time, although I should have taken a clue from the fact that Mama had five of us. I didn't stop to wonder how I would have loved two at the same time had my wish for twins been answered. I was just thankful that I was alive and well and had a baby of my own at last.

One thing I heard from my friends who were not as new as I to the hood was how much having a child impacts one's life. As Mama had not drummed this into me over the years I was not inclined to hear it.

Girly, parenthood changes your life so completely!

I want you to hear and prepare for it. From the shock of hormonal changes that cause such a wide variation in emotions; crying for no comprehensible reason, to indiscriminate throwing up, all without regard for the cost and quality of one's clothes. Then just when you think you have a handle on this parenting thing, the child begins to talk and question 'Why?' to everything.

Over the years, my friends and I have talked about the manual that should have been passed on to us before embarking on our own experience of bringing up children. Mama forgot to pass on the manual and she was so many miles away from my life and my initial experience that I had no one familiar to make reference to.

I am grateful for some great literature and resources by Focus on the Family[18] and

Care for the family[19] that helped in our navigation of some of these roads.

The areas that these resources were unable to help with had to do with my cultural understanding and background and how we had learned from our parent's example how to raise children.

This raising children thing is an education in itself and is not taught in school! Perhaps the reason they did not teach parenting at school was because they would never have space for all the different manuals required to cover all the variables that come with every single child.

I started off with this cute little female who though very determined did not shout so loudly and could not throw a fast ball if her life depended on it. Next came this more pliable but noisy and ball-throwing boy. The principles I had learned to help me bring up my girl did not always work with my lovely new bundle.

Dr James Dobson of Focus on The Family
has published a book on Bringing up Boys[20]
and I think it is a great idea and resource, as
the differences in bringing up boys and girls
as well as in bringing up one child after
another require an expansion in the mind of
parents.

Where this doesn't occur it can lead to a lot
of damage and trauma in the children's and
a parent's lives.

One of the first signs of parental trauma that
I had to deal with was related to breast
feeding. This was the single main experience
that fuelled my determination to write down
some information for my daughter to be able
to refer to, as needed, in her journey in life.

You see I knew that all good mothers breast
fed, both by observation and hearing it said
over and over again to Aunties and friends
and anyone else who sought help from my
Mama and Grandma. What Mama never told

me was that it could initially be painful process.

In addition, she wasn't there to guide me through it so for a week after having my girl I was in agony, but to be a good Mum I persevered. I admit that breast feeding was a wonderful part of bringing up my children but I now understand totally why some mothers choose not to pursue this route, and would not dare consider them bad mothers.

My hungry girl kept feeding correctly at my breast till I was so sore I could not wear a nursing bra. The thought of ever letting her go near me again was so agonising, that eventually I called a midwife and explained that I would like the hungry crying child to be bottle fed from then on.

She was lovely, explained that my milk "hadn't come in", that I should leave my breasts bare and allow them to heal in the open as I had blisters caused by my baby sucking in vain. She said that I would live to breast feed again and that it was not always going to be a painful process.

She took baby away and returned with her content and full. This occurred in the two days in which I was in hospital after giving birth.

I breast fed both of my children happily till they were ready for solid food, but would have liked know in advance that it would cause me pain, which with a little understanding and perseverance would lead to the useful start that breast feeding is for children.

I must prepare you for 'first blood' especially if it is oozing from the fore head. I cannot recall the details of how my toddler ended up with a bleeding injury to her head, what I do recall is the amount of blood that was pouring out and just wouldn't stop. I frantically called a friend for help, and she experienced mum that she was very quickly laid my anxiety to rest.

You see, I had determined that this was not a huge gaping gash, and my friend talked me through cleaning it up and explained about the amount of bleeding being normal especially with forehead grazes in little ones.

She explained the technicalities which I cannot recall for the life of me, but I was so relieved that no permanent damage was done. There is now not only no scar to show for that experience, but there were to be further occurrences of injury that did not result in life long damage to either me or the children.

In this information era where children as young as ages 10 and 11 are giving birth to their own children, I don't think the issue of where children come from and how they are made is a big mystery anymore. Parenting is not for wimps and it is definitely not for children. Most parents will tell you that even they did not feel adequately equipped for the task once faced with it.

Un-protected sex not only potentially leads to sexually transmitted diseases, it also leads to unplanned pregnancies and ultimately unplanned parenthood, that is if both parties are even able to accept the responsibility.

As a result of the information era in which we now live there is plenty of useful material; parenthood classes and resources that can help to prepare one for their own journey into parenting, as well as see them through the process.

My Mama used to say, *"To be fore-warned is to be fore-armed."*

My cousin had a lesson in raising children from my children who were both under 12 at the time. They suggested that she think carefully before having children and suggested she should not have too many as it wasn't an easy task bringing up the two of them never mind having more than two.

In West Africa, when we get married, the prayer that you have tons of children is usually greeted by hearty amens.

I am grateful to God that he answered my prayer for not one but two sets of twins by giving me none. In the days when families lived in close communities of extended family, raising children was a shared experience. As our world changes, a lot of energy and skill is required for the job of parenting which has become less a community effort, which my children can testify to.

We don't just have and raise children for the sake of it or because that is what our upbringing has taught us, but we want to have blessed and resourceful children who will stamp their mark in a positive way on our lives, their society and generation.

The constant changes in our daily living create different child care dynamics than what they had in Mama's day. While I was growing up, there were very few Day Care Nurseries. Today, they are a thriving business and replace the foster care that was more prevalent in my time. As a result, the values and standards that our children learn may be a mish-mash of all those involved in their primary care.

'Train up a child in the way she/he should go and when they are grown they will not depart from it' [21] the Bible advises and I say if you want your child to reflect your values then make sure you teach them these. Make the time and plan your life style to ensure it happens.

Sons are a heritage from the Lord
Children a reward from Him [21]

MY WISHES

CHAPTER 9

Rice, Yam and Roasties

Oh no I can smell burnt rice...again! I cannot recall the number of times I burnt a pot of rice! If there is anything I ever needed counsel for it was the trauma that resulted from being asked to prepare plain boiled rice for mealtimes. I had a reputation for burning rice and was often scolded and jibed for this.

The most amazing thing is that I took up a career in catering. So I wish Mama had told me that it was just a matter of ratios....

I have deep rooted memories of spending useful play hours picking over and washing rice in order to remove   stones and other debris that used to be found in sacks of rice in those days. Then I would have to cook it: Horrors!

That rice can be successfully cooked by adding the appropriate amount of lightly salted water (not hot) each time in the ratio of 2 of water to 1 of rice, bringing the rice to the boil and then turning the heat down to simmer for 15 to 20 minutes before going out to play, would have been such a life saver.

Ah, don't get excited yet because there are different types of rice from wild rice through to basmati, jasmine, red, glutinous to name but a few, but it is still only a matter of knowing the ratios and following the simple steps for long grain to achieve rice perfection: no more burning or over cooking.

Basmati: two of water to one of rice, jasmine 1 of water to two of rice. Check pack instructions or go to the web or ask mama for cooking times of the different types of rice.

It helps also to know not to cook endless amounts of rice but that 60g to 100g per person dry weight is sufficient. Even if you choose to get a rice cooker which will eliminate the need for you to stand around watching the pot, you still need to be aware of ratios to get perfect cooked rice.

Have you ever gutted a fish? How I dreaded market days as inevitably there would be fresh fish in quantity needing to be scaled and gutted. I have the scars from those days to prove it, even if not physical all my dreams of becoming a hand model were put paid to after I encountered those fins.

I am sure they were not meant to be removed and the gills certainly had no desire to be separated from the fishes' heads.

I wish I had known that de-scaling and cleaning fish does not have to be such a hard and dangerous undertaking, especially if you are armed with a sharp pair of scissors and knife. Alternatively, buy them de-scaled and cleaned or pay the extra needed for someone else to do the job.

We loved celebrations or occasions because there was always bound to be 'moin-moin' or steamed bean loaf. Well, maybe everyone else looked forward to these celebrations but this was another occasion for my hand model dreams to be squashed, as in order to provide this divine delicacy, oodles of black eye beans had to be de-skinned.

It seemed that the only tool able to achieve this with any measure of success was a large grater. The problem as I saw it was, during the hours it took to complete a batch; a large portion of the skin on the fingers would be removed and washed away with bean skin debris.

Once again simply knowing that you could save time, dreams and fingers by buying pre-peeled beans is a good thing. Failing this, the beans can be soaked in water for about twenty minutes till just before they have fully absorbed all the water and their skins are stretched taut. This makes removing the skins by rubbing between the palms of the hands, less of a chore, but a chore nevertheless.

I thought a scotch bonnet was a pretty hat worn by Scottish ladies. I wish Mama had warned me about the other type of scotch bonnets. It was another nice, sunny market day and may have been close to the Christmas season as it seemed like we had double of everything including the scotch bonnet peppers.

These had been tossed into a large bowl then filled with water and my task was to wash them, separating the useful from the bruised. About an hour later with most of the job concluded, without a whinge, I add, my hands began to tingle and then throb all over.

I was released from duty when the pain showed no sign of abating. I washed my hands with all kinds of substances and tried some local remedies including using palm oil, ice and even petroleum jelly, fondly called Vaseline.

I wish Mama had told me the effect chillies – yes, also known as scotch bonnets - can have when in contact with human skin. It would have saved me heading out for a disco that day dressed in the latest boob tube with my hands stretched out in front of me in need of endless airing as they throbbed endlessly.

It would have helped to know beforehand that chillies should be handled with care or at least with rubber gloves dedicated for chilli work and never allowed to come in contact with any part of the skin.

It seems like most of my 'hands on' experience around food was gained on market days. I came to dread those days and looked forward to being elsewhere but Mama always ensured that I stuck around as these were also training days for my future.

Have you ever heard of a bitter leaf (*Veronia amygdali*)? Well there is one that has culinary uses, actually there may be several but there is one I know of that is great as part of a sauce, but some of the bitterness has to be extracted by washing severally before use.

Maybe it is my imagination or faulty recollection but this job also seemed to be mine to perform on a consistent basis. Problem was it was not my remit to determine when it tasted just right, had it been I would have been done after the first few washes.

As an avid catering student in later years, I discovered that green vegetables do not have to be washed three million times in order to remove debris as this results in destroying nutrients present in the vegetables.

While I enjoyed eating yams I never looked forward to the preparation beforehand. We used to buy huge yam tubers which I always thought resembled a chunky tree root. In order to cook the yams, you had to first peel off the outer layer of bark. This would be fine if it were the new yam season as yams harvested during this season had very flimsy skins.

My recollection is that most of the yams I had to peel were tough old tree roots and the knife never wanted to separate the thick skins from the succulent white tasty flesh. I watched others perform this task and they made it look simple.

It was during catering college, years later and having discovered a swede; (also known as Neeps in Scotland, Rutabaga in America and is a root vegetable of the cabbage family), a filleting or flexible bladed knife and a chopping board that I made a connection and wish Mama had spared me the agony by introducing me to these bits of kitchen equipment much earlier on in my yam peeling journey. There is nothing like having the appropriate equipment for any particular job.

Ogbono soup! This was one of those delicacies my father looked forward to. The basis of this delight was a flat cream coloured seed with a tough brown skin.

The first issue with this sauce was that the outer skin of the seeds needed to be removed in order to make the sauce authentic, and secondly you needed several hundred seeds per pot of sauce.

So Nana, this being Mamas Mum or my Grandma, decided it was time for me to learn how to cook this particular sauce in preparation for my future in my husband's house, and it was Ogbono day on the dreaded menu.

Having spent well over an hour patiently scrapping off the brown layer of skin with a sharp knife, Nana proceeded to give me verbal instructions on how to cook this delight without taking her eyes off her Singer sewing machine.

Off I go and proudly prepare this sauce which turns out black and without the texture that it should usually have. Those who are familiar with this soup know that its authentic colour is not remotely close to black.

This was my first experience of the virtues of visual learning in relation to me, I discovered I learn better when I watch something being done, than solely from spoken instructions. Daddy was gracious and ate the sauce with praise for his novice cook, but I was so embarrassed to discover that there was a vital step in which the seeds, once ground to a fine powder had to be fried in hot palm oil to release its properties and textures.

I'm not sure Nana mentioned this and Mama certainly wasn't in on the lesson that day. Now, had I been able to watch the process while someone else was cooking, things may have turned out differently that day.

You can make the perfect roast potatoes before you are thirty years old. Simply peel the skin, using a sharp knife or potato peeler, add to a saucepan of cold water and bring to the boil. As soon the water begins to boil turn the heat down to a slow simmer and allow the potatoes to boil for about eight to ten minutes. Drain and shake them around in the pan gently just to roughen the surface.

While the potatoes are boiling, pour enough oil in the base of a roasting tin and place the tin in a pre-heated oven. Add the shaken potatoes and roast till a rich golden brown colour is achieved. Serve and delight those you are feeding.

If concerned about using too much oil lightly spray the shaken potatoes with spray oil instead for similar results.

The easiest and most economical way to peel potatoes is using a potato peeler. With practice it can also become the quickest.

Pre-heat the oven to 200°C to 220°c for best results. It took me years to know this.

It is legal and OK to prepare Eba (cassava granules) pronounced (Ehh-Baa) in a saucepan, this being another authentic growing up culinary delight. Everyone I watched added the granules to freshly boiled water in a bowl and seemed instinctively to know when there was enough.

In my attempts though, every time I made Eba, it was either too soft or too hard or not cooked through and this was unacceptable. I wasn't encouraged to make it in a sauce pan, neither was I given quantity measures, and I discovered I lacked the instinct.

In later years as a homemaker I would get my other half to make the Eba especially when we were expecting company, until I discovered that I could better determine consistency and texture by cooking it in a saucepan and stirring as I went along. I also found this made a lighter end product. In fact, go one step further and prepare your Eba in the microwave.

Mama had not suggested that it was ok to modify or veer from traditional methods or if she ever had it was one of those days when I wasn't listening.

It is by experimenting, modification and error that many recipes where born, so I say even traditional recipes could benefit from a bit of tweaking. Live a little: experiment!

Cooking is a pleasurable art if you understand what you are doing. Don't spend zillions of hours preparing food to the exclusion of all else, that is unless you really want to. It is amazing how the right tools can make cooking even more pleasurable and if it helps, watch someone perform a skill before you try it out for the first time. That's what you tube seems to be created for...watching.

Take Mama's oral recipes out of your head and write up your own perfect cook book for consistent results each time. In other words, take oral tradition and extend its useful life, and if packaged nicely you may even be able to give these away as gifts.

Make sure you give the gifts with the corresponding tools! This mama will have to provide her girl a hand book of her recipes.

If the axe is dull and its edge unsharpened, More strength is needed But skill will bring success.

MY WISHES

CHAPTER 10

The Rock

I remember like it was yesterday standing in my cute pink and white kaba (a type of dress popular in Cameroun), that had been made for me by Nana as everyone fondly called my grandma.

We were outside in the compound, (the area surrounding the buildings that comprised our home) Nana in her favourite over stuffed square leather chair and I having been summoned to her side to sing again for her, what was her favourite song that she particularly liked to hear me sing.

Christ is my rock, my refuge, my stronghold,

Firm as the trees route that clutches the land, He who has faith builds without worry, Not like the man who builds on the sand, I set my house on a solid foundation, Christ is my rock the route of my soul's recreation.[24]

At the time, I was about 11, and this song meant way more to Nana than it did to me, as I did not understand the language of some of it.

Over the years, I have come to be found singing my heart out in these words no longer just at Nana's request, but because this has become the truth and statement of my life.

If there is any final word I could leave to mine and any other girlie to remember above all else, it would be the truth conveyed in the words of this song.

The following ten things are just some of the ways I have discovered how stable a foundation The Christ has been in my life.

Through head wrenching pain: I recall headaches starting out unannounced and without warning in the year after I finished my senior school exams. This pain would be located on one side of my face and through my eye and felt like someone was pulling my head in one direction.

Sometimes, to compensate I would lean my head into the pain, so it appeared like I was walking lopsided. Visits to doctors and several different treatments and suggestions later, I was no better. If anything they were getting worse.

I have since learnt that these where a type of migraine. At the time and in the place I was, no one was able to provide a solution to the pain and there was no evident rhyme or reason to when it would strike.

I called on the Rock out of my despair, pain and hopelessness. Every time one of these would strike I began to repeat to myself some truth that I had learnt in church about Christ being my healer and my hope. This was the only thing that brought relief.

Eventually, after about a year of dealing with the debilitating headaches in this manner and seeing a reduction in occurrence and duration I was finally set free from this pain and have never since had headaches of this kind. This was the first of many such experiences of healing where all else had failed, this sustained my life and sanity over the years.

Through temptation: There are some things we get to better understand and more readily define as we get older. I was about seven years old and a new nanny had been employed to assist with the care of us five children.

I recall that this nanny while giving me a shower would play around with my private parts creating a sensation I found not unpleasant but unsure was acceptable.

This was the beginning of my introduction to a struggle with lesbianism which continued till I was about 13. I somehow knew they were wrong and hated trying to fulfil these longings. I found that when the longings came I would do things that normally would not be acceptable to my conscience.

I never told anyone about this struggle I had and recognised that if I continued like this something strong and powerful and outside of myself would control me and I didn't like being controlled this way.

Again, I cried out to the God my Mama and Papa had introduced me to through our catholic upbringing.

I can't say that this went away immediately but over the years I learnt about temptation, doing something that I really didn't want to but that provided a certain amount of perverse satisfaction and pleasure.

I learnt through step by step training and looking at the Word of faith what the line in that song meant about he who has faith building without worry.

My dark secret created such anxiety in me and I remember the moment I realised I was finally free from this pull that dragged me to a place that I never really wanted to be. No one but my Rock could be attributed to freeing me from a pattern in life that I never really was content pursing and that would have eventually led to my demise.

In today's society, our Nanny would be accused of child abuse but in those days what was being done to me was not something commonly spoken of, acknowledged or recognised.

At about that age in my life, I started my own search to learn more about this Rock that had been introduced to my thinking through my catholic upbringing, but who was not held in the position of esteem that I was beginning to think He should be.

Through depression: It started when I was pregnant with my girlie and continued till she was about 2 years old. With hindsight, I realise it was post-natal depression and resulted in hair loss, overweight and the fact that I never wanted to get out of bed. If I had been in the habit of drinking before that time I'm sure I would have turned to the bottle, but as my search for the Rock up to that time had led me to give up alcohol, I turned and shouted, screamed, cried out to God for help again.

When I look back at that time I see how often God had tried to answer and help me but I didn't hear or was unable to respond. Finally, I heard a prompting that reminded me of how I had been set free in the past of something that seemed to be dominating me, by which I had no desire to be controlled: familiar pattern.

In the mornings on those days when the house was emptied of all human life form except me, and just before I gave and went back to bed, I would put on a tape of a preacher and fall asleep listening. After some time of doing this, I began to gain the strength to live again.

During this time, I was attending church regularly but not hearing a word that was spoken.

Again, through a process that took me to going to a Christian conference in Birmingham, England I came fully alive again. The hair loss stopped, the asthma that I had been diagnosed with sometime during that period declined and the weight gain began to be reversed.

I came to realise through spending time and talking with the One who had become the root of my souls recreation that I had been depending on everyone else but Him and unfairly so as only God is infallible and only

He is solid like the trees root that clutches the land.

Through aloneness: I mentioned in an earlier chapter that there was a time I emigrated from my familiar surroundings and country to a land I was told flowed with milk and honey. One of the down sides to this move was that while it may have had milk and honey, it did not have my friends or family in it, nor was the culture familiar and I had just taken this life altering step.

There was no one to navigate me through the unfamiliar terrain of marriage, an introduction to the job market, no one I could talk with about new feelings, desires, and longings. No one I could ask for tips on marriage and why some of the things I had expected were not turning out to be so and how I should deal with them.

Again I turned to Nana's Rock, that was now my Rock through experience and relationship.

I think it would take a whole epistle to communicate the things He took me through and how. Not only did I survive an utter sense of aloneness, I came to value time alone, I learnt to dig roots in dry places and thus found that my foundations where beginning to head in the same direction as the trees root that clutches the land.

There are so many books on the market and so much information on the web covering topics from money management to time and household care.

But when I started to build my own home there was not so much information readily available, there was not the wiser mentor to guide me through and when I left home someone had omitted to give me my manual for daily living.

A search through my programming revealed that the state of my life up to that point was as a result of what was stored in my mind and reality was proving that this was insufficient information for successfully navigating life.

I called upon the Rock who had seen me through to date and asked for help with mundane things like running a home, managing my time, cooking for one, two and then four, running a household and a list of other activities that I found myself unable to successfully juggle.

Never once, did I not receive an answer. I set up schedules for myself around the areas that were of concern to me as directed, in answer to my prayers. I was given step by step instruction on how to do this. Usually, a short way down the line, I would come across a book or article suggesting what I had done as the solution to a particular life dilemma and my information had come through direct communication with my Rock.

I stopped marvelling after the third or fourth occurrence but was more certain than ever that the Rock I depended on was indeed my refuge and my strong hold.

If there is any guide in life that is dependable and sure it is the Rock of my salvation.

Over the years, I have had step by step guidance on finding lost things and people as well as guidance to the solutions to current dilemma.

There are so many of these but one that occurred when my girlie was a little older comes to mind and which she may recall.
One of the uncles had visited and it was time to go home. For the life of us we could not find his keys and we had searched all sorts of conceivable and inconceivable places.

As is usually the case just before frustration began to set in, I called on the Rock for help. A few minutes later I felt the urge to go looking in the garden. I could not understand this as it didn't make any sense how a key that had been placed on a table in doors could be in the garden.

You see my little man had the habit of hiding things at the ages of 3 and 4, and we had searched through his room and interrogated him thoroughly to no avail. So, having learnt from experience, I headed off into the garden in the early sunset and began a search.

This time though, I was listening to the inner voice for direction and felt the need to go and retrieve my sons bicycle helmet from the washing line where someone had hung it up. He had been playing with this and some sticky tape earlier making a comfortable place for one of his superhero toys to pass the time.

As I began to unravel this, what should fall out but the errant car keys. Somehow they must have got stuck together while he was busy, as when questioned again he could not remember knowingly storing them away in that location. Uncle was grateful and got home safely that evening, and I marvelled once again at the prodding that had lead me this and many other times to discoveries that otherwise seemed impossible.

I am always open to hear that guiding voice these days which I recognise above the other voices and sounds in my world as a result of my long term relationship with the Rock of my Salvation.

I walked into the office like I had done before to say good morning before going to teach my class. The office manager wanted to know what was going on with me as I looked so alive and well and was positively beaming with health and loveliness. I have had this reaction on and off over the years.

I finally realised that it coincided with times when through life's busy schedules and demands, I had made the time to communicate one to one for extended periods with mine and my Nana's Christ. I always seemed to come out glowing internally, to the extent that people noticed the glow on my face.

I have also learnt that life and living seem to throw everything in the way to seemingly prevent one from experiencing such times.

I have never been high on alcohol or drugs but when people talk about a high I can relate that to times of being so close to God that I come out with a spring in my step and a sparkle in my eyes. After such times I am ready to take on the world.

If I had life to do all over again I would make times with The Rock a priority over everything else. As it is I have to train myself to not respond to every little impulse that is seeking my attention and suggesting the next urgent thing, rather to take the time off to relate intimately with my Saviour as He is the basis of my life and the length of my days.

Wisdom has been defined as the ability to correctly utilise knowledge and apply understanding.

After all this time I am beginning to realise that all the direction that has been given me in living life has been to bring me to the point of wisdom. I don't know or understand everything, therefore I still have a lot of wisdom yet to acquire.

I finally realise as stated in the bible, wisdom is the principle thing. In getting to know God as my Rock, I have had to read His Word daily and constantly and listen to His voice and know now that the greatest wisdom comes from Him.

It has taken me my lifetime to date to find this out and if I can get my girly to get a hold of this truth from now, I am setting her up for a life lived with understanding, making choices based on the wisdom of God rather than on the dictates of the world, the flesh or any other dominating forces or even, on her own understanding.

I am not suggesting a life without knocks but that you will be infinitely better equipped to face the knocks. Also that those things that are vital in your life will not to stolen away by ignorance as you will be able to deal with them better.

Everyone needs this Rock that they can hold onto through the storms of life. The Christ of my Nana that I was introduced to early in life has seen me through so much that it goes beyond coincidence.

So I am passionate that my daughter and any other girlie should get to know Him early in their life's journey. He will never leave you nor forsake you and even when you can't make sense of the storm He is there and will see you through. And when eventually you look back on your days you will be able to sing with me, 'Christ is my Rock, my Refuge, my Stronghold....'

This one thing is clear, though my Mama did not know all the things that perhaps would have helped to make my experience of life less eventful, she did take me to church and began in me the process that was to introduce me to the Rock of my life.

Without the relationship, the guidance, the ability to cry out to Him, His being there for me, comforting me, helping me and a myriad other descriptive terms I could find, I would not be today.

So, Mama left me the best legacy of all and now I pass this on to my girlie and others, in a form that is retrievable.

Go and grow into the life that you were born to live, free from fear and compulsion from any source other than the loving gentle leading of the Rock.

Love,
Mama.

MY WISHES

.

APPENDIX 1

Favourite Foods list guide.

Feel free to add yours

1. Basmati rice with goat curry and vegetables
2. Beef bourginion/ beef goulash
3. Beef cobbler
4. Beef or vegetable lasagna or moussaka
5. Beef/lamb stew casserole) with dumplings
6. Bobotie with golden rice
7. British stews: Lancashire hot pot, beef stew, Irish stew
8. Chickpea curry
9. Chill con carne with jacket potatoes
10. Coated drumsticks with mash and frozen vegetables
11. Coq au vin with roasties
12. Couscous with roasted veg
13. Egusi soup with mixed meats and pounded yam or ground rice

14. Enchiladas and salad
15. Ewa/bean pottage with naan bread or dodo
16. Fennel baked fish with basmati rice
17. Fish fingers, burgers and fries
18. Fried rice with coated chicken wings and hot salsa
19. Groundnut soup with chicken and ground rice
20. Homemade pies: steak and mushroom, chicken and veg, potato, lamb with mash, veg and gravy
21. Homemade pizza and chips
22. Jerked steak roast veg's and potatoes
23. Jollof rice with chicken, mixed veggies and dodo or beans
24. Lamb biriyani
25. Lamb with apricots
26. Mash with steamed fish, parsley sauce and veg
27. Meatballs (chicken, turkey or beef) with pasta and a tomato sauce
28. Ogbono soup with pounded yam or potato fufu and beef

29. Oxtail potjie (curry) South African style
30. Pasta carbonnara with turkey ham
31. Plain rice with fish stew and dodo
32. Pork plait with three vegetables
33. Potato and lamb curry
34. Quiche with salad
35. Rice and peas with curried lamb or chicken
36. Risotto with roasted vegetables
37. Roast: Beef/Chicken/Lamb with roast potatoes and two veg
38. Rosemary chicken with tagliatelle
39. Salmon fish cakes with mash and white sauce
40. Sausage and mash with onion gravy
41. Seafood okra soup with Eba
42. Shepherd's pie with peas and sweetcorn

One of these favourite foods lists could be drawn up for breakfast and lunch items also.

APPENDIX 2

Assign a food type to a day for example;

Sunday: Roast dinners Lamb, fish, beef, chicken...
Monday: Rice
Tuesday: Pasta
Wednesday: Naija food
Thursday: International, try a new dish
Friday: Something with fries/chips. Keep it simple
Saturday: Leftovers

Other options could be vegetarian foods, vegan foods, Potato dishes, eating out or take away and so on.

APPENDIX 3

Weekly menu guide built from favourite foods list:

	Breakfast	Lunch	Dinner
Sunday	Cereals	Leek and potato soup	Roast beef, potatoes, Yorkshire pudding, 3 x veg
Monday	Pancakes with syrup	Seafood chowder	Chicken wings paella
Tuesday	Oats	Lentil soup	Tagliatelle carbonnara with turkey ham
Wednesday	Crumpets with cheese	Moroccan harissa	Ogbono soup with Eba and mixed meats
Thursday	Eggs (omelette) with bread	Chicken soup	Special chow mein

| Friday | Baguettes with bacon | Roasted vegetable soup | Pizza and chips |
| Saturday | Yogurt with muesli and fruit | Tomato and basil soup | Left overs |

Other lunch time options could be sandwiches, toasties, salads...

It may be an idea to swop and have the heavy meal at lunch time and the lighter lunch ideas at dinner time.

If you have an infant this just needs to be modified and tweaked a little and you need to buy a really good hand blender and storage jars, and they can also partake in family meals.

You can modify the ideas depending on the size and ages of your family and their dietary needs.

When you sit down to do this, once you have all the information to hand, it takes very little time to draw up a menu for the next thirty days or even for the next quarter.

APPENDIX 4

Grocery shopping list:

Based on your weekly menu you are now able to devise a shopping list and at some point you may want to consider a monthly shopping list if you have the storage space, it's a tool to save money:

Packet cereals	leeks
Ham	potatoes
Beef joint	4/5
different vegetables	
Syrup	Lentils
Chicken wings	yogurt
Baguettes	bread

And so on based on your recipes.

I will mention that every kitchen should have what I call store cupboard must haves, a collection of basic grocery items that are used regularly. These can include frozen items e. g. frozen vegetables, chicken wings, milk, homemade stock etc. Dry store items like sugar, flour, tea bags, coffee, onions, milk, eggs, oats, spices, herbs, rice and the list goes on. This will have to be catalogued in another volume for my daughter!

There are several apps that can be used to record shopping list and weekly menus if you are that way inclined.

APPENDIX 5

Cleaning schedule

Like all the guides above you need to modify this to your own living space.

Spend about thirty minutes each a day on hoovering or sweeping up generally, the same with dusting and clearing away. Put on a wash if you need to.

Break down you house into sections, for example:

- Living dining room   LR
- Kitchen K
- Toilets and bathrooms TB
- Garden G
- Bedrooms B

Week 1: Concentrate on one of the sections above and do a thorough clean. Say the living room is the chosen section, then you have a list of all the areas that need cleaning and take on the tasks one at a time through the whole of week 1 in thirty-minute time frames.

Living Room-LR areas to clean for example:
Cobwebs
Dust-furniture, pictures, window sills, chairs
Vacuum- floor, chairs, lamps shades, side stools
Wipe- leather chairs, skirting and window sills
Clean- windows, lampshades, doors, radiators, fireplace
Tidy- games basket, remote controls basket
Week 2 Kitchen

Week 3 Bedrooms etc.

Till all the sections have been through this thorough cleaning cycle over five weeks or however many sections you have. Doing this in a regular cycle will ensure that you space never gets out of hand and limits the need for a daily frantic spurt of activity to get it clean. No need for frantic cleaning just before visitor's arrival.

Also based on this you will be able to determine what products you need to add to your shopping list for household cleaning.

If you have to take a break from this schedule for any period of time you can do so without stress knowing that your spaces are under control, that you can come back to the schedule and also that you can ask others to do little jobs here and there just to keep things under going.

END NOTES

All Bible quotes are taken from The New International Version NIV unless stated otherwise

1. Prince Nico Mbarga, 1976. Sweet Mother. Online at:www.waado.org Accessed 3rd April, 2015
2. Hunt, M. 2014 Debt Proof Living. Revell, A Division of Baker Publishing Group
3. Foster, H. 2002 Dejunk Your Life. Aurum Press Ltd
4. Bach, D. 2002 Smart Women Finish Rich. Broadway Books (A Division of Bantam Doubleday Del; Rev Ed
5. Ecclesiastes 10:19
6. Oxford Dictionaries. Language Matters. Online at: www.oxforddictionaries.com Accessed 3rd April, 2015
7. Williamson, M. 1992. A return to Love: Reflections on a Course in

Miracle. Harper Collins, Chapter7, Section 3 (pg190-191).

8. Proverbs 18:16 King James Version
9. Proverbs 8:10
10. Coyle, N. and Chapian, M. 7 Oct, 1994. Free To Be Slim. Kingsway Publications; New edition
11. Proverbs 31:30
12. 1 Corinthians 13
13. Psalm37:4
14. Cilley, M. 2007 Sink Reflections. Random House Publishing Group
15. Psalm127:1
16. Chapman, G. 1 Dec 2009. The Five love languages. Moody Press
17. Amos3:3
18. www.focusonthefamily.com
19. www.careforthe family.org.uk
20. Dobson, J.C. 2014 Bringing Up Boys. Lifeway Christian Resources
21. Proverbs 22:6
22. Psalm127:3
23. Ecclesiastes 10:10

177 Things I wish my mother had told me!

24. Winter, T. (Sr) Christ is My Rock.
    Medical Mission Sisters found on the
    web

Let us start the manuals that we can pass down to the following generations, I have left pages blank within this book titled *'my wishes'* for you to record your own thoughts and pass these down to the next generation.

To support some of the ideas and suggestions in this book there will be 100 recipes and things about them handbook to follow.

There are also things I want to share with my son so in typical 100 things manner there will be 100 things from a Mama to her boy. So look out for these titles!

Enjoy your journey.

Printed in Great Britain
by Amazon